IMAGES
of America

LEWISBORO

IMAGES
of America

LEWISBORO

Maureen Koehl

ARCADIA

First published 1997
Copyright © Maureen Koehl, 1997

ISBN 0-7524-0545-4

Published by Arcadia Publishing,
an imprint of the Chalford Publishing Corporation,
One Washington Center, Dover, New Hampshire 03820.
Printed in Great Britain

Library of Congress Cataloging-in-Publication Data applied for

Contents

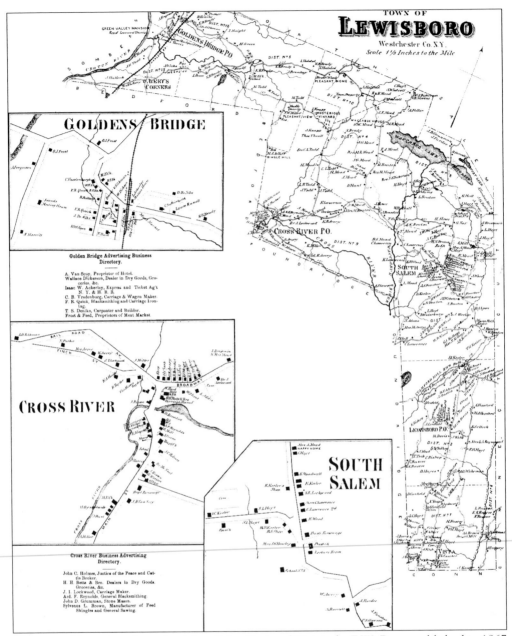

This map of Lewisboro from the *Atlas of New York and Vicinity* by F.W. Beers, published in 1867 by Beers, Ellis, and Soule, illustrates what makes Lewisboro unique. Former Supervisor and Town Historian Alvin Jordan noted the "shotgun" shape of our town. It is 17 winding miles from east to west, with six distinct hamlets or population centers and four separate post offices. The village clusters, separated by acres of farmland, are apparent on this map. Missing are the twentieth-century changes like the reservoirs that so drastically altered the lives of Goldens Bridge and Cross River residents, and the improved highway system that enabled city folk to choose all of Lewisboro as a fine place to live.

Introduction

Lewisboro is a town of unpretentious beauty. A rural area 50 miles north of New York City, it has remained a Westchester backwater even though it is one of the fastest-growing communities in northern Westchester County. There are six hamlets in Lewisboro: Goldens Bridge, Cross River, Waccabuc, South Salem, Lewisboro, and Vista. Each hamlet has retained a distinctive personality throughout the 260 years of the town's existence.

Nature has endowed the area with beautiful lakes, sparkling streams, and the rock-strewn fields common to New England. To the north, Long Pond Mountain with its rocky cliffs stands tall, and nearby rises the highest point in Westchester County (about 965 feet), but most of Lewisboro's 28 square miles are rolling hills punctuated by rock outcroppings.

Although Lewisboro is part of New York, much of its eastern half was once part of Connecticut, and many of the settlers in that section came from the Connecticut shore towns. The western half of the town was first settled by the tenant farmers of Van Cortlandt Manor, most of whom migrated into the area from the vicinity of the Hudson River and points south.

The enigma of our town's name remains unsolved. When the town was first settled in 1731, it was known as Salem and covered a rather large area. In 1783, the area was divided into Upper Salem and Lower Salem along the rocky ledges above Long Pond. In 1788, New York passed a statute establishing towns, and the Van Cortlandt Manor section became an official part of the town of Lower Salem. Then, in 1806, the name of our town was changed again, this time to South Salem.

In 1840, John Lewis, a wealthy gentleman who was born in the eastern section of town and may have lived here as a young child, offered South Salem the tidy sum of $10,000 ($7,000 in cash, $3,000 in railroad stock) to improve its public schools. The catch? The name of the town must be changed to Lewisboro. Mr. Lewis, a resident of New York City, was very interested in the modern idea of public education. Why did John Lewis choose our town for his generous gift? The reason is not clear, but his mother's family was prominent in Vista and his uncle was a school board member.

All these name changes had little effect of the day-to-day affairs of the citizenry. Each hamlet continued to carry on in its own independent manner. Goldens Bridge suffered the joys and the heartbreak of improved transportation beginning with the appearance of the railroad in 1848. A little over one hundred years later, the era of the super highway brought with it six lanes of concrete that divided the hamlet in half and wiped out much of its character. But Goldens Bridge residents are proud of their hamlet and a strong sense of community exists today in Old Goldens Bridge, where some residents live in houses their families have occupied for generations.

Cross River, on the other hand, was miles from the railroad and the multi-lane highway, but it also suffered the pangs of progress. Much of its village and the farmland along the Cross River disappeared under the waters backed up by the building of the Cross River Dam in 1905. Rebuilding some its shops and houses on higher ground, the hamlet continued as a farming community until the 1960s.

Waccabuc, nestled near the pristine lake of the same name, has witnessed little change over the passing years. Mead Street, the center of the hamlet, was settled by the Mead family in 1776 and continued under Mead influence for almost two hundred years. The hamlet boasted a post office and a school but no businesses, except those of the gentleman farmers. Known far and wide as a place of beauty, it became a summer vacation destination. Today many of the Meads are gone and the farms have been replaced by a golf course and new homes, but the special ambiance of the hamlet remains.

South Salem has always been the governmental center of Lewisboro and the most populous hamlet. The surrounding area was dotted with small, self-sufficient farms which were served by the hamlet's merchants, blacksmiths, millers, and tradesmen. Many farmers supplemented their incomes by making shoes during the long, cold winter months. After the Great War, farms started to break up and several lake communities were developed, bringing newcomers to town, mostly as summer residents. As the years went by, the summer residents became permanent residents and the population began to grow. It remains little changed, a twentieth-century Brigadoon.

Lewisboro Hamlet is the hardest to define in terms of its physical boundaries. In the 1860s it had a post office, school, church, general store, and several grist and sawmills. Spread out along the highway to New Canaan, Connecticut, the land was predominantly given over to large dairy farms and small family farms. With too small a population to support the store, post office, and school, any semblance of a community center disappeared. Today no farms remain. Where once cows grazed and corn waved in the wind, there are housing developments and manicured lawns, although the feeling of the open fields remains and there is a strong sense of community.

Vista, the hamlet on the eastern border of Lewisboro, was an active community with several general stores, a post office, a couple of churches, a school, a shoe factory, and a small quarry. There were mills in the area to serve the farmers. Located just a few miles from New Canaan, other services were available there. Vista is another hamlet that has maintained its links to past generations. A few families still live in the old family homesteads. Over the years, the shoe factory and all but one of the original stores have disappeared. The church is no longer used as such and the post office is a private home, but the hamlet is being revitalized by a large new supermarket and a few small businesses. The farms have been replaced by houses but the enduring spirit of Vista persists.

This book is an attempt to illustrate a significant part of Lewisboro's history through the photographs and memories of a few of the town's families. The earliest photographs were taken just after the Civil War. They begin our photographic journey through the next one hundred years.

Some of the photographs are from the town historian's collection, but many others were generously loaned by historically-minded families from each hamlet. Though the pictures came from only a few longtime residents of Lewisboro, they portray the daily comings and goings and the special celebrations familiar to all of us. This generosity has added much to the history of the town we all are proud to call home.

One
Goldens Bridge:
Farms, Rails, and Roads

Of all the hamlets in Lewisboro, Goldens Bridge has had the most change forced upon it by influences beyond its control. First came the reservoir at the beginning of the twentieth century, and then the tide of concrete highway in the last half of the century. Walter Harrison took this panoramic photograph of Goldens Bridge in 1939 from what is now the parking lot of the A&P shopping center. The railroad station is in the center, and Mandia's water tower is just visible to the south of the Sheffield Creamery buildings. At the time, Goldens Bridge was still a busy railroad depot, but after World War II, many changes took place and this scene disappeared forever. The entire area, as far as the railroad tracks, is now under the concrete of Route 684.

The railroad came to Goldens Bridge in 1848, creating changes for the hamlet's residents. Powerful locomotives pulled carloads of passengers, mail, and freight through the town. The arrival of the railroad put the stagecoach lines from White Plains and Sing Sing into a decline. Farmers welcomed the rail service, and dairy farms prospered with an efficient way to ship their products to New York City.

The second Goldens Bridge station was built *c.* 1890. Four tracks can be seen in this 1920s-era photograph. The tracks in the foreground, dating from 1872, split off toward Lake Mahopac, a popular tourist spot. The last train to Lake Mahopac ran in 1959. Goldens Bridge had several hotels and guesthouses popular with summer tourists, as well. The houses in the distance are bordering Route 22.

Nodine's Hotel and the firehouse are the two closest buildings in this old view of what later became downtown Goldens Bridge. The empty space between the hotel and the firehouse in later years was the site of the A&P and Senior's Pharmacy. The camera is looking south along Route 22, still a dirt road at this time, from the vicinity of the railroad tracks.

Green Brothers' crossing, where Route 138 crossed the railroad tracks, was the scene of too many close calls. This time the truck lost to the train, and the gentlemen walking the tracks are investigating the May 1941 fatal accident. The truck's tires are leaning against the building. Goldens Bridge's unguarded crossings presented constant hazards for farm vehicles, foot, and automobile traffic.

Once known as Callahan's Hotel, this gambrel-roofed house was one of the buildings moved in 1903, when the land was flooded for the Muscoot Reservoir. The Callahan family ran the inn and tavern, which were popular with visitors during the summer. Fishing in the nearby reservoir was a popular lure for tourists. The house has been owned by the Palmer family since 1923.

Belly up to the bar, boys! Drinks are on the house. This bar in the Callahan Hotel dates to the early days of the twentieth century. Locals and travelers staying at the hotel spent many a social hour swapping tales of "the ones that got away" and discussing local politics. The taverns' barstools began to take the place of the general stores' pot-bellied stoves.

A quartet of happy fishermen proudly shows off their best catch of the day in front of the Callahan Hotel. Fishing in "the lake," as the Muscoot Reservoir is called by the Goldens Bridge old-timers, was a favorite leisure activity that provided supper as well!

Hot times were had in the old firehouse hall on Route 22 during the Roaring 20s! Here, a family poses on the steps of the firehouse in their party clothes. Note the right-hand drive on the open roadster. The firehouse was built in 1911. It was demolished in 1965, when the new quarters were built on Route 138.

Some of these happy young folks are just plain tired of smiling for the camera! Ties seem to be the order of the day for the gentlemen, while the girls are dressed as perfect young ladies in the fashions of 1923–24. Walter Harrison is the second from the left in the first row.

This modern, two-room schoolhouse on Old Bedford Road was opened in 1912, replacing the 1893 building behind it. The older building was "beyond repair." The new school was used until 1955, when the students were sent to the Katonah Elementary School. In 1963, Increase Miller Elementary School opened, and Goldens Bridge children returned to their own hamlet for their education.

Obviously, the Goldens Bridge Campfire Girls have been up to something theatrical! This photograph may have been taken in the Methodist church hall, the firehouse, or in the school. From left to right are (front row) Doris Comings, Millicent Hoyt, Helen Anderson, Hortence Brady, Marjorie Anderson, Eleanor Smalley, Ruth Comiskey, Mary Leonard, and Marguerite Palmer; (back row) Mary Colgan, Eleanor Rowan, Velma Cole, Clara Smalley, Julia Todd, Sarah Archer, Alice Comings, and Lucille Rowan.

Goldens Bridge was just a wide spot in the road to travelers going north and south on Route 22. Sometimes called "Dodge City," its several blocks boasted seven bars, a couple of butcher shops, a unique storefront A&P, and a couple of gas stations. Senior's Pharmacy had a soda fountain, and the gas stations sold legal fireworks for the Fourth of July.

The A&P of the 1940s and '50s, under the management of Jack Benish, was famous for personal service. Dry goods, canned goods, and a little fresh produce were sold, but no meat. However, Mr. Benish would take an occasional meat order for a customer, drive to the Katonah A&P to fill it, and have it ready the same afternoon or the next morning.

Koopman's Meat Market did not do any business on this March 1956 day! Heavy rains caused extensive flooding of Route 22 in the Goldens Bridge business district. Scenes like this were common after big storms until the roads were regraded in the late 1950s.

Floods in this hollow where Route 22 met Route 138, near the ball field, seemed to be a yearly event. This March 1956 photograph was taken near Green Brothers' Store looking south. No through traffic today! Route 22 was the principal north-south highway before the coming of Route 684 in the early 1970s. This pre-Revolutionary roadway was the New York to Albany Post Road.

Cutting ice was an important winter task in every community. The Palmer family posed during a break from ice-cutting in the reservoir's Second Cove. Squares were scored in the ice, and the scored area was lined with planks. The blocks were then cut with a saw and floated between the planks to the skids on the shore.

After the ice was at least 12 inches thick and could stand the weight of the equipment, it was ready to harvest, or cut. The Palmers cut the ice by hand until the 1920s, when the gas-powered saw was introduced. The block ice was hauled up the skids pictured here onto the waiting horse-drawn wagons and was then taken to the icehouse.

In this photograph, ice from Muscoot Reservoir is being stacked in the Sheffield Milk Company's icehouse near the railroad tracks. After the ice was brought to the icehouse, it was covered with hay or sawdust to insulate it. The milk company went out of business about seventy years ago, but the icehouse is still used as a storage shed by King Lumber.

Life around the railroad tracks could be hazardous, especially when sparks flying from passing locomotives landed in the grass or on someone's roof. In 1909, a group of men organized the Goldens Bridge Fire Department. It is the oldest of Lewisboro's three fire departments. The first fire engine was the horse-drawn vehicle seen here. By 1913, horse power had been replaced by the gasoline engine.

Green Brothers' General Store was one of the hamlet's gathering places. Owned by Caleb and Edward Green, the store had everything from fish hooks to kerosene for lamps and coal for the furnace. Farmers came from as far away as South Salem to buy supplies at Green Brothers'. The store closed its doors forever in 1964, when the era of the super highway came to the hamlet.

Goldens Bridge had its share of wealthy families and large estates, along with the dairy farms and small family farms. The Guirey riding academy, Boots and Saddles, on Todd Road, had an elite local clientele. In this 1946 photograph, we can almost feel the brisk November air and sense the excitement of the hounds as a hunt gets under way. The riding stable closed about 1953, after the death of Colonel Guirey.

Goldens Bridge has its own balanced rock. It is located in a wooded area off Route 138. The huge boulder sits on a hillside a short distance from a stream. Not quite as spectacular as the North Salem Balanced Rock, it is, nevertheless, deserving of recognition. Is the rock a glacial leaving? Or is it a dolmen erected ten thousand years ago by Celtic visitors?

Originally a cow barn on George Todd's farm, this barn is one of the focal points of the Goldens Bridge Colony. The barn was home to a day camp during the week and provided a gathering place for dancing and entertainment every summer weekend. Older residents recall the early days when cows resided downstairs. Great fun was had by the youngsters jumping into hay thrown from the hayloft.

In the formative years of the Goldens Bridge Cooperative Colony, the women carried the community during the week. They ran the day-care center and the summer camp, planned cultural activities, and held fund-raisers for myriad causes, local and worldwide. Development began in 1927. At first, families lived in tents while they built their homes. Country living for these workers and professionals offered a respite from the city's pressures.

An enthusiastic group of teenagers posed during a break c. 1939. They were helping the stone mason build a retaining wall at the colony's beach. From left to right are Phil Friedman, Jerry Zakheim, Teddy Wishnefsky, Heshy Kladel, Dave Bergh, Sam Friedman, and Mac Arons.

The lake in the Goldens Bridge Colony has always been a focal point of summer activities. It was once a ravine with a brook running through it. In 1938, two dams—one earthen, the other concrete—were constructed to contain the water. An 8-acre lake was created, providing a swimming area for the residents. Old-timers remember fox hunts scrambling through the ravine before it was flooded.

Lake Katonah was another vacation community in Goldens Bridge. The clubhouse, seen here, was built in 1927. Homes were nestled into the hills surrounding this 25-acre lake. Developers Ward, Carpenter & Company purchased 125 acres from the Brady estate in 1926 and enlarged the existing lake. Lake Katonah was advertised as a summer recreational community that was away from the trials of summertime in the city, but still an easy commute for the breadwinner.

Dig these 1928 fashions! Competition was keen in the early days at the Lake Katonah Club. Spectators came early to get a good seat on the boardwalk next to the clubhouse. Some of these racers show better starting form than others. Watch out, Number Four!

The men had to get into the competition, too! Canoe paddles were good for more than just getting from one end of the lake to the other. Here we see a fierce struggle for supremacy at the Lake Katonah Summer Games. Besides water activities, there were tennis tournaments, barn dances, dinner dances, and masquerade balls. The men's swimming costumes weren't any more glamorous than the ladies' in 1928.

This photograph of the Somers Highway Bridge was taken close to a century ago, when preparations were being made for the flooding of the land along the Croton River by the New York City Department of Water Supply. Note the increased length of the span anticipated by the building of the New Croton Dam in 1895. The railroad trestle (not visible in this photograph) is south of the bridge. At least half a dozen Goldens Bridge homes and farms were taken by the flooding of the Croton River valley caused by the damming of the river. As devastating as the flooding was, the residents appreciated the waters of the new "lake." Fishing was a favorite activity, and most Goldens Bridgers loved to fish and to picnic on the shores.

Two
Cross River: The Crossroads of Lewisboro

This pastoral sight greeted travelers from Katonah as they made their way down the hill into the hamlet of Cross River about ninety years ago. The large white building on the right is Fifth Division Market (formerly the Hunt General Store). The lake in the foreground was meant to provide fishing and recreation for the villagers during the warmer months and ice for cutting in the winter. However, a small retaining dam was built farther upstream than planned and over the years the area has silted in. Now only a small stream flows through a wet piney grove just west of the Fifth Division Market.

John Hunt's store was one of the buildings that succumbed to the rising waters of the Cross River Reservoir in 1908. Long a gathering place for the local farmers and village residents, the general store boasted the usual pot-bellied stove, hardware, and dry goods associated with rural living. The store was dismantled before the flooding and rebuilt on the site of the present Fifth Division Market.

The George Monroe family lived in this house on Old Shop Road. George is standing next to his home in this 1903 photograph. Notice the rain barrel at the front corner of the house underneath the gutter. Rainwater coming off the roof was collected in the barrel for household use.

The first Methodist Episcopal congregation in Cross River was organized in 1843 by the Silkman family. By 1850 the church had been built. The congregation was served by a circuit minister who also served the Goldens Bridge Methodists. This 1906 photograph shows the church in its original location before it was moved to the east side of the highway to make way for the flooding of the Cross River valley.

"The Pines" was the home of Dr. James A. Breakell, the first "non-native" to be elected town supervisor (in 1892). He was the only Democrat to hold this office until Robert P. McGreevy was elected supervisor in 1995. An unpublished Van Norden manuscript states, "A brisk campaign in 1893 [elections were held annually] restored the office to the Republicans and to our old families. Not until after the turn of the century did the strong feelings and some bitterness thus aroused dissipate."

The Cross River Baptist Church, built in 1791, is the oldest public building in town. Subscription money totaling £130 was raised to begin construction on the 36-by-30-foot meeting house. An 1855 addition to the south end of the church included the steeple and the bell gallery. Church suppers and Sunday school were held in the gallery.

Even today, Cross River Baptist Church retains the New England charm seen in this picture taken on Easter Sunday in 1901. The church was a gathering place for the hamlet, with an active Sunday school and Christian Endeavor Society. In the beginning, services were conducted by a visiting minister from Connecticut, or by laymen like Joshua and Gideon Reynolds.

In the boom years following the Civil War, railroads were the future! Dairy farmers were eager for access to a line. If all the railroad schemes had been successful, Lewisboro would have been crisscrossed by at least three lines. The New York, Housatonic and Northern was to connect White Plains to Brookfield, Connecticut, following the path of Post Road through Cross River and Waccabuc.

This view from the highway, taken just south of the Baptist church looking north, is long lost to the flooding of the Cross River *c.* 1907. Cross River was a country village "composed mostly of shoemakers and basketmakers," according to the builders of the reservoir. The three homes pictured here belonged to Augustus Pullen, George W. Hunt, and Frank E. Reynolds.

George Avery was a prominent shopkeeper in Civil-War-era Cross River. His building was once an emporium providing Cross River families with household goods, fancy items, clothing, and lampshades. There were bins galore for kids to rummage through for odds and ends. About 1860, Avery suddenly closed the doors to his shop, never to open them again. Some say he mourned the death of his wife; others hint the closing was in protest to the election of Abraham Lincoln and the taxes he imposed. Only George Avery knows why he let the building slowly collapse over the next forty years. A peek through the rotted boards in 1906 revealed a cellar stocked with merchandise, hat boxes, and hoops and balloon skirts hanging from the ceiling.

Before the coming of the reservoir, George Hunt, brother of store owner John Hunt, operated a grist and cider mill on the Cross River. The mill stood near the present entrance road to Pound Ridge Reservation. The mill was a popular place for farmers to bring their grain and apples. Cider was a favorite beverage hereabouts. Many times, the frolics and square dances were enlivened by the flavorful and sometimes potent beverage.

All you need is a sunny day, a reason to celebrate, and a camera to catch the moment! These Cross River folks have come together for a family picnic, one of the favorite pastimes of the early twentieth century. Perhaps they are swigging some of Scott Piatt's locally bottled beer and cider from George Hunt's mill.

Grandpa George W. Reynolds, Uncle Harrison, Cousin Elsie Reynolds, Helen and Mabel Silkman, and Edwin Reynolds (from left to right) pose for a 1920s-era Reynolds family photograph on the hay wagons. Time to give the horses a rest. Horses provided the farmer's plowing and haying power into the second half of the twentieth century.

This fork in the road looks a bit different nowadays. Ed Smith's blacksmith shop on the Katonah Road (in the center of the picture) is still standing and is now the bait shop. The left fork is Old Shop Road, but the fence, wall, and tree are long gone, victims of the reservoir flooding. The right fork was called Railroad Avenue for a while, but the trains never came and the name disappeared from town maps.

The Cross River landscape changed after 1905, when the New York City Department of Water Supply claimed the hamlet for a storage reservoir. About thirty-two buildings were affected. Several dwellings were moved to higher ground nearby, or as far away as Katonah. Many were demolished or taken down, and the lumber was used elsewhere. A cement bridge replaced the old bridge, and the road was realigned. Just visible in this c. 1906 photograph, taken before the total flooding of the reservoir, is the mill dam, all that was left of George Hunt's grist and cider operation. The Baptist church sits on its hill, and just visible in the far background is the Methodist Episcopal church, recently moved to its present location near the Brick House.

The waters of the reservoir finally gave rebirth to the hamlet. After the lake had filled behind the dam (about 1908), new stores and businesses settled in and life went on, along with the new century. By the 1920s, motorcars were a common sight as day travelers began to discover the charms of Lewisboro. Note Hunt's General Store with the gasoline and kerosene pumps that have replaced the hitching posts.

"Spirits of Water, Earth and Sky, All gather here, Where once dwelt one who like the spring, Was sparkling, sweet and clear." So reads the inscription on the Bailey Fountain placed at the Cross River crossroads about 1910 by Dr. Pearce Bailey as a memorial to his wife. The Bailey home, now known as Four Winds, is a private psychiatric facility. The fountain was a favorite resting place for travelers.

36

Frank Scofield, Frank Webb, and Robert Leal (from left to right) take a photograph break and lean against their Westchester County truck filled with some mighty large logs cut from the Pound Ridge Reservation property in the early 1920s. These logs are probably bound for Pa Whitman's sawmill on Boutonville Road.

Pa Whitman and his crew are hard at work cutting the large native hardwood logs into boards. The portable saw was powered by a gas engine, but the entire apparatus had to be pulled by a team of horses to wherever it was needed.

Cutting ice from the Cross River reservoir was an important winter task. Cross River old-timer Martin R. Silkman (1903–1997) remembered, "You had to push the snow off before you could cut, and the ice had to be 11 to 12 inches thick before you could cut it . . . and you could cut ice every winter." Bill "Pa" Whitman and crew are loading blocks onto the trucks for the journey to the icehouse.

William Whitman Sr., better known as Pa, operated a sawmill on his property on Boutonville Road just outside the present entrance to the Pound Ridge Reservation. The area abounded in maple, beech, birch, oak, and pine trees. Here we see Clinton Tripp perched on a sled full of logs. The snow made easier going for the horse-drawn sled.

The Bleeker family lived in an eyebrow-window style early-nineteenth-century home on Boutonville Road. This family photograph was taken around the turn of the century. The Bleekers operated a garage-repair shop on Route 121, just north of the Methodist Episcopal church. The garage is still standing but is no longer in business.

Pa Whitman, bounty hunter, poses with his catch! Foxes were considered "vermin" in the 1930s, about the time this picture was taken. Pound Ridge Reservation Superintendent Whitman and his dogs, Blackie and Susie, seem to have rounded up a sizable number of vermin! Foxes and chickens didn't mix, and the eggs were more valuable to area farmers than the foxes.

Chapman Miller (1887–1950) lived in Cross River all his life. He ran the Hunt General Store before moving several doors east in the 1930s and opening his own bake shop, which served as the post office as well. Chappy Miller was the postmaster until his death. His daughter, Ruth Rohner, succeeded him. Miller was a pillar of the Cross River Baptist Church. He published many of the postcards used in this book.

"Snowed all night—and blew a gale. Roads are blocked. Two/three cars came here from the west. Nothing from the east. No mail today and no school. Town snow plows out of commission. Men busy digging drifts. One car was stranded last night up by Roses'. Vance rescued the man about 5:30. Colder tonight. Clear but wind is blowing." This entry was taken from the diary of Postmaster Chapman Miller for February 20, 1934, the date of the photograph.

Barely visible in this 1902 photograph of young Cyrus Russell and his father, H.W. Russell, is a field where the reservoir is today. The pile of pumpkins resting against the brick house attests to the fertility of Cross River soil. Russell homestead produce was sold locally and taken to Katonah by wagon for sale in the markets.

Hazel Zarr and Cyrus Russell (1897–1971) were married in 1922. The stylish young couple paused along the roadside to have their picture taken. Cyrus Russell served Lewisboro as town clerk for twenty-four years and supervisor for eight years. The Cross River schoolhouse, now the Community House, was named in his honor when he retired as supervisor in 1970. Hazel Russell died in 1994.

The Brick House is a Lewisboro landmark. It was built in 1829 by Gideon Reynolds of bricks made from clay found on the property. It boasted seventeen rooms and twelve fireplaces. This stately brick house replaced a smaller home that stood closer to the highway. "Old Gid" operated the stagecoach that ran between New York City and Danbury, delivering mail and passengers, from the early 1800s until 1849, when the railroad put an end to business along the New York to Hartford and the New York to Burlington Post Roads. Reynolds's stagecoach made two round trips per week. The fare from the Bowery to Cross River was $1.62 $^1/_2$ (half-pennies were in use then); $1.75 to South Salem; and $2.25 to Danbury. The Brick Tavern, as the Reynolds' home came to be called, was 49 miles from New York City. A stone mile marker used to stand along the highway opposite the house. Gideon Reynolds was Cyrus Russell's great grandfather.

The Brick House took in boarders after much of Cross River's land was condemned for the impending reservoir. Mrs. C. Reynolds welcomed summer boarders as well. In the 1920s, Mrs. William Mae ran a "high class inn" known as the Edna Mae Coffee Shop. After World War II, the Brick Tavern was owned by the Jensen family, who ran an inn and restaurant until they sold the property to Elinor Merrill in the late 1950s.

This photograph was taken on April 4, 1915, Easter Sunday, from the front of the Brick Tavern on Route 121. The newly formed Cross River reservoir offers a serene vista, and, unlike today, the view is not interrupted by pine stands and tree-covered hills.

Curtains in the windows make the Cross River one-room schoolhouse look mighty inviting. In 1866, the trustees and voters of the school district resolved to raise $1,800 to build a new schoolhouse with two privies, a fence, and seats. The old one was in such a state of disrepair that it was cheaper to build this "new" building. Electric lights were installed in 1916. The school was used until 1940. It is now the Cyrus Russell Community House. This photograph was taken c. 1895.

Company 210, Camp SP-9 of the Civilian Conservation Corps, established in 1933 as one of Franklin D. Roosevelt's WPA projects, was home to two hundred young unemployed men from all over New York state. Camp Merkel was run with military precision. The young men lived in these barracks, the foundations of which can still be seen, in the Ward Pound Ridge Reservation. Local church socials offered diversions to the CCC men.

Camp Merkel was a semi-permanent installation at Ward Pound Ridge Reservation from 1933 to 1941. The men worked hard at construction, reforestation, and reclamation projects within the park. All of the lean-tos, the Trailside Museum, and many of the park masonry projects were accomplished by these men, who received a pittance for their labor and had to send most of the money back to their families during the Depression.

Annie O'Neill had a farm on North Salem Road, just south of Todd Road. She was a remarkable woman who was often seen driving her milk cans by horse and wagon to the dairy in Goldens Bridge. During the 1930s, she would hire hobos and wanderers to help with the haying and other farm chores. According to Leslie Bouton, Annie was not above "doctoring the cider to get them to hoe her corn!"

The O'Neill sisters' farmhouse survived at least a century, but fell into disrepair as the years wore on. The sisters managed a small herd of cows and eked out a living, but, by the 1950s, the house was a derelict and was burned down by the South Salem Fire Department in a practice drill. The foundation stones can still be seen if one looks hard enough.

Today the evergreens tower over the Fifth Division Market. Anthony Felice took over the "new" Hunt General Store in 1938 and named the store in honor of his World War I army division. Just after World War II, he went into partnership with his son, Ralph, and Ralph's high school buddy, Waldie Gullen. Ralph and Waldie bought out the senior Felice's share in 1949 and continued the popular grocery store for thirty years.

Fifth Division owners Felice (left) and Gullen (right) attempt to drive away the "Blue Law Blues" by playing cards. Forbidden by the authorities to sell meat on Sunday after a complaint was lodged by a rival shopkeeper, they lost some of their brisk business supplying lunches for hungry Sunday hikers and fishermen in the nearby county park and reservoir. Eventually, the storm blew over, and the Sunday blue laws were changed.

47

Times had already started to change in Lewisboro even though this 1927 photograph of the divergence of what was then Route 123 (now Route 35) and Pinchbeck Street (Mark Mead Road) still evokes a sense of the slow-paced country life. Although Cross River remained a farming community for two more decades, developments in the lake areas of South Salem were beginning to bring people and traffic to town. Not until the late 1930s was the highway straightened and paved to accommodate the increased traffic. The hamlet of Cross River survived the dam and the flood, and the reservoir actually attracted visitors with its beauty. Westchester County had recently established a large county park, the Ward Pound Ridge Reservation, in its midst. Cross River was truly becoming a crossroads.

Three
Cross River Dam:
A Mighty Wall of Stone

Great changes came to Northern Westchester County in the 1890s. Its neighbor to the south, New York City, was in constant and ever-increasing need of clean, potable water. Therefore, the aqueduct commission began to improve and enlarge the Croton Reservoir system. The construction of the Cross River Dam was part of that plan. The towns affected were not pleased with the decision to build the dam and hopes were high that engineers would not find a suitable rock foundation in the area. However, in February 1905, the aqueduct commission announced that the dam would become a reality. Properties along the westward flowing Cross River, between the hamlets of Katonah and Cross River, were condemned. In Goldens Bridge, farms and dwellings along the Croton River were also taken by New York City authorities, and the people were forced to move to higher ground throughout the broad river valley. In this photograph, taken in 1906, construction of the dam is nearing completion.

The flume chute seen in this postcard view was an important component of the dam-building process. By means of this conduit, the waters of the Cross River were allowed to flow, uninterrupted, during the construction of the dam. Note the buckets lying on the rocks underneath the flume. Buckets were used to transport building materials.

In this postcard view of the area west of the planned Cross River Dam, the Cross River can be seen flowing toward Katonah and its junction with the Croton River. In the foreground, the rails used by the narrow-gauge railway that carried supplies from the depot in Katonah are visible. This rather rickety railroad was nicknamed "The Boutonville Express." It frequently toppled over, to the vast amusement of area residents.

Work on the dam has progressed in this view. The gatehouse tower appears almost completed. The gatehouse controls the release of the reservoir waters. The gates allow the water to be released at different levels depending upon conditions. Work on the dam began in June 1905. According to the *Katonah Times* of July 14, 1905, "hundreds of Italians are at work clearing the land where the big dam will be built."

Here is a part of the Cross River Dam the public rarely has a chance to observe. By 1908 the eastern wall of the dam was covered by the waters of the newly formed reservoir. Within the gatehouse an iron grid traps flotsam before it flows into the dam. Behind the bars are the actual gates of rolling steel, which are raised and lowered to control the water's flow.

The MacArthur Brothers Company was the dam contractor. The *Katonah Times* of June 30, 1905, reported "next week a force of 400—500 southern colored men are expected." The workers began to build a mile-long track from Elliott's Lumberyard in Katonah to the site. A trestle was constructed across the "flat" and the river. The tracks ended at the height of the dam near the stilted buildings seen in front of the derricks.

The derricks visible in this postcard view supported wires used to transport buckets filled with cement, tools, or quarried stone to the work stations. Several buckets are overhead in this picture. Note the mule and wagon in the foreground. In June 1905, two railroad carloads of mules and drivers arrived at the site and were established at the George Green Stock Farm, east of the dam site. The farm is now under the reservoir.

Wintertime has arrived and thousands of pallets of quarried stone are covered with a blanket of snow. Some of the stone may have been quarried near Peekskill, where stone for the new Croton Dam had been obtained. Two hundred Italian stone workers were brought in to construct the Cross River Dam. They lived in shanties along the railroad tracks in Katonah and in a camp town near Mt. Holly Road.

In this 1920 photograph of the dam and spillway, all looks peaceful, and the fountain aerator is bubbling gracefully. In October 1955, the same horrendous storm that washed out bridges and roads throughout the area caused havoc here. The *Katonah Record* for October 20, 1955, reported that "waters from the Cross River Dam spillway carried off most of the new brick pumphouse at its base."

The lakes and rivers of northern Westchester had been considered as a potential water source for New York City since the 1830s, and, indeed, a dam was completed on the lower Croton River in 1842. It wasn't until June 1905 that work actually began on the Cross River Dam. The dam's gates were closed on August 7, 1907, and the waters began to accumulate.

All was not as serene during the dam's construction as it might appear in this c. 1910 postcard view of the roadway across the dam. The *Katonah Times* for July 14, 1905, reported that a cook had stabbed a worker in the Mt. Holly Road camp. In 1906, the Mafia moved into the shanty towns, terrorizing the workers. Several murders transpired. A sheriff's headquarters was set up at the dam site to protect the workers.

This *c.* 1920 photograph was taken from the dam looking west toward the village of Katonah. The Cross River is wending its way west to join the Muscoot Reservoir. Peace had returned to the Cross River valley, but the area would never be the same. Some villages were destroyed; others, like Katonah and Cross River, were moved to higher ground. A number of homes, barns, and businesses in Goldens Bridge were moved or dismantled. The Cross River Dam is 840 feet long, 170 feet in height, and 330 feet above sea level. The storage capacity is 11 billion gallons. The cost of the dam was $777,741.

By 1907 or 1908, when this photograph was taken, the waters had collected to form the beautiful Cross River reservoir. The reservoir is just over 3 miles long. It is a mile wide at its widest point, but the shoreline is very irregular. Alvah P. French's *History of Westchester County*, published in 1925, described the reservoir's setting as "country surroundings—somewhat wild and generally rocky." Before the flooding, the hamlet of Cross River was a typical farm community with the usual complement of shoemakers and basketmakers. It was served by several general stores, a couple of mills, and two houses of worship—the Baptist church and the Methodist Episcopal church. After the building of the dam, the mills were gone, some of the shops were gone, and a number of families were gone, but the spirit of Cross River remained to rebuild Lewisboro's crossroads.

Four

Waccabuc and the Three Lakes Area: From Camps to Castles

Lewisboro's beauty is reflected in its many lakes. Perhaps the most fabled of these lakes is Waccabuc, the one the Native Americans called Wepac or Wecquapaug, meaning "at the far place" or "at the end of" in the Algonkian language. The white settlers translated the strange-sounding word to "Long Pond." In the 1850s, when the Waccabuc area was promoted as a vacation paradise far away from the ills of the big cities, the name Long Pond was replaced by the more romantic sounding Lake Waccabuc. In this *c.* 1890 photograph, taken from the Mead Street end of the lake, the hills of Connecticut close in about the lake's eastern shore.

From the dawn of man's presence in the three lakes area, Lake Waccabuc has been a place of serene beauty, offering solace and solitude, sustenance and recreation. This picture, taken almost one hundred years ago, could have been taken today, as canoes remain a favorite way to explore Waccabuc's mile length.

From this perspective, one can imagine the rolling pastures and hayfields of the self-sufficient farms of the last century. The large building on the shore is the Waccabuc Hotel boathouse. To the north, Castle Rock towers 100 feet above the crystal surface of Lake Waccabuc, challenging the brave and the foolhardy to plunge from its heights into the clear water. This photograph was taken by David I. Mead in the late 1800s.

Lake Waccabuc provided its share of winter entertainment. This group seems to be making sure the ice is thick enough for an ice-skating party in this 1911 snapshot. Later, there will be a roaring fire near the boathouse, with hot chocolate and other good things to refresh the spirit!

What is more reminiscent of an old-fashioned winter in the country than a horse-drawn sleigh? Sleighs were the most efficient manner of transportation once the snows had come. This family may be out for a pleasant afternoon ride, or they may be on their way to Sunday church services in South Salem.

Sarah Frances Studwell Mead stands in the formal gardens of Tarry-A-Bit, the home that she and her husband, George Washington Mead, built in 1895. Sarah was an avid gardener with an interest in flowers and vegetables. One can imagine the fragrances wafting from this magnificent garden on a warm summer's day. The couple had twelve children; eleven reached maturity. Most of the children settled on Mead Street with properties of their own, thus perpetuating the Mead family dominance of the area for another generation. After George W. Mead died in 1899, Sarah Mead built the Mead Chapel in his memory. Members of the family donated items to outfit the beautiful fieldstone chapel designed by Hobart Upjohn.

Golf certainly was a popular summertime leisure activity for the residents of Mead Street, so why not get a little practice in on the expansive lawns of Tarry-A-Bit? About 1913, a group of enthusiasts formed a golf club, leased a bit of land, and engaged John Gullen to design the first nine holes of a golf course. A new era had begun!

These ladies were friends of Frances S. Mead, the oldest daughter of George W. Mead and Sarah Studwell Mead. They are members of the "Reading Club." This photograph was taken to commemorate the occasion of the club's 44th anniversary on June 5, 1931. Tredinoch, the gracious home of Frances Mead, is just visible in the background. The house was built in 1917.

In 1776, newlyweds Enoch and Jemima Mead came on horseback from Greenwich to set up housekeeping on land given to them by Enoch's father. Enoch's younger son, Alphred, built this home in 1820. Eventually, the property came to be known as The Homestead. In this very early photograph from the late 1860s, the members of the household are enjoying the afternoon sun and the comings and goings of Mead Street.

Milestones were placed along the major roads as early as 1771. They marked the distance from Federal Hall in New York City. Lewisboro was a crossroads for two post roads. These roads diverged in Waccabuc at the Mead Street intersection. Continuing north on Mead Street led to Bennington, Vermont. Traveling east along the road to Ridgefield brought the sojourner to Hartford. This mile marker on Mead Street reads, "52 miles from New York."

There were several large farms along Mead Street. They supplied the needs of each family as well as the neighbors. A closer look at this photograph, taken sometime after the Civil War, reveals quite a bit of activity. One gentleman appears to have just arrived on horseback, and three young ladies are hurrying down a quieter, less traveled, Mead Street. Perhaps they are making their way home from school.

The schoolhouse on School House Road was built in 1894 by Robert Hoe. This class photograph was taken in November 1937. From left to right are (sitting on the front step) June Reardon, Marley Marseilles, Howland Adams, Billy Marseilles, Timothy Smith, and Harvey Adams; (middle step) Helen Heron and Pebble Stone; (back step) Peggy Dibble, Dorothea Cudgna, Waldie Gullen, and Bobby Dibble.

In the early 1860s, Martin Rockwell Mead converted his Mead Street home into a hotel he called the Waccabuc House. After his death in 1882, his wife continued to operate the hotel until it burned in 1896. Waccabuc House offered city dwellers respite from mosquitoes, malaria, and other curses of city life in the summer. Guests came by train to Goldens Bridge, then by stage or foot to the hotel.

The Waccabuc House boathouse stood at the western end of the lake, just east of the hotel. The dappled pathway beneath the gently swaying trees beckons us toward the pleasures offered within, whether it is to go for a row or a paddle around the lake, or to try a hand at bowling on the boathouse alleys.

The Lake Waccabuc Post Office was built in 1894 by Robert Hoe for the benefit of the growing number of families on Mead Street. The mail came from Ridgefield and Katonah in a four-seated carriage with a team of horses driven by Charley Ruggles. The Waccabuc post office has continued to be a source of pride for the hamlet for over one hundred years.

"This way to Lake Waccabuc Inn," indicates the road sign. These three gentlemen look rather pleased in their shiny automobile. The Robert Hoe mansion, now Waccabuc Country Club, on Mead Street was converted into the Lake Waccabuc Inn c. 1913. The inn offered rooms and meals and marvelous country weekends away from the hustle and bustle of the city. The newly-formed country club offered golf and tennis to its members.

This family group posed for a picture in 1910, probably at the Benedict-Knapp farm on Benedict Road. Three generations are represented: Mrs. Jonah (Mary Brady) Benedict, her daughters, Ruth B. and Laura B. Knapp, and Laura's daughters, Ethelyn and Mary Knapp. Buff, the dog, is smiling for the camera, too. Benedict land extended along the south shore of Lake Waccabuc and along the south shore of Lake Oscaleta as well.

The two ladies in the canoe are obviously dressed in their Sunday best for a paddle on Lake Oscaleta around the turn of the century. Lake Oscaleta was known as South Pond until 1895. It is not as deep as Lake Waccabuc, its neighbor to the west.

In 1925, Samuel Dickens built a store by the Waccabuc-Oscaleta channel bridge. He sold soft drinks and snacks to boaters. In 1929, he moved his business to the northeast end of Lake Waccabuc, where he built a boathouse on wood pilings. His son, Merwin, took over the business in 1945 and ran it until 1960, when he converted the boathouse into his year-round residence.

Sam Dickens purchased this log cabin from George Ruscoe in 1923. The Ruscoes had attempted a similar boat rental and store, but could not compete with the Dickens's business. It is hard to believe that this gas station actually existed on Cove Road, in a quiet summer community! The fuel was sold to boaters and motorists using the Dickens's facilities.

Although the back of this photograph states, "Mrs. Florence, whose husband worked for Richard Lawrence as a caretaker and rented this house from Mr. Lawrence," this appears to be Jim Florence, himself. The Florence family lived in the house for many years. The house, a classic New England saltbox, is now owned by the Cowles family.

This happy ensemble is posing in the side yard of the house pictured above. The property, at the west end of Lake Oscaleta, was known as Camp Clover and was the scene of many a merry summer gathering. In 1892, at the time of this photograph, the house was owned by John Howe, a friend of Richard Lawrence, and was rented to "campers" during the summer.

Camp Clover was the place to be in the "good ol' summertime"! Just ask this formal foursome. In 1902, the property was transferred to R.H. Lawrence. Guests were always welcome, the more the merrier! Badminton, swimming, minstrels, and tennis kept the revelers busy during the hot summer days and nights around the turn of the century. Mr. Lawrence stayed in his elegant new home across the lake, away from the noise of the campers.

At Camp Clover, age made no difference! Guitars, banjos, hats, and a talent for dressing up to have a good time were the only ingredients needed for a weekend of fun. A century ago, everyone played a musical instrument or knew how to sing the popular tunes of the day. Notice the "clover" badges worn by many in this group. The gentleman in the top hat is probably Richard H. Lawrence.

In the early decades of the twentieth century, camps appeared along the shores of Lakes Oscaleta and Rippowam. This 1921 photograph shows the cottage of J. Franklin Ryan, a prominent Katonah resident and Bedford judge. In a previous life, it had been a North Salem schoolhouse. Judge Ryan hauled the schoolhouse over the mountain on a horse-drawn wagon and rebuilt it as his summer camp.

Not only did cottages spring up along the lake's shores, but many families had boathouses as well. The sprightly Judge Ryan is seen building his boathouse on the south shore of Lake Oscaleta in this 1927 photograph. He maintained his camp until 1947. J. Franklin Ryan died in the 1980s, at the age of 105.

In 1892 Richard H. Lawrence built this home, which he called Oscaleta Lodge, at the eastern end of South Pond. He renamed South Pond "Oscaleta," meaning "little kiss" in Spanish. In 1924, Mr. Lawrence enlarged his home to create the structure shown in this photograph. The property was purchased by James Abrams in 1951.

Peering out from Marion Holden's boathouse at the eastern end of Lake Oscaleta is a group of World War I army veterans, friends of Miss Holden. The picture was taken c. 1930. The boathouse was built by Miss Holden's uncle, R.H. Lawrence, in the early 1900s. The boathouse has been moved and is now the caretaker's cottage on the James Abrams' property.

Called Sarah Bishop's Rock when the photograph was taken in 1890, this outcropping is more often referred to as "Sarah Bishop's Cave." Sarah Bishop was a hermitess who frequented the area about the time of the Revolutionary War. She is said to have lived in this cave for almost thirty years, until she died of sickness or exposure during a storm about 1810. Her cave sits back from the boulder-strewn cliff on the north shore of Lake Rippowam. Sarah Bishop was a religious person and attended the Church of Christ in Salem. She occasionally did domestic chores for the villagers. Her origins are unknown. Sarah may have escaped from the British occupation of Long Island, or she may have belonged to a local family. Sarah Bishop's Rock was a popular destination of nineteenth-century picnickers as evidenced by the dated graffiti on the cave walls.

This home (bottom) was built in the 1930s by Charles and Alice Mead Neergaard. It is called Gaardhouse and sits on a hillside overlooking lower Mead Street. Across Mead Street can be seen the buildings of the Alphred Mead Homestead. Alice Neergaard was very active in town affairs, especially the District Nurses Association and the World War II civil defense effort.

The Port of Missing Men was built atop the mountain separating North Salem and South Salem about 1907 by Henry B. Anderson, who owned much of the mountainside overlooking Lake Rippowam. For several years, the teahouse was very popular. About the same time, Mr. Anderson built a twenty-room mansion overlooking the lake, but he abandoned it within a few years, leaving it to fall in upon itself.

The Indian Ovens are one of those mysteries Mother Nature produces for us mere mortals to solve. Located in one of the coves of Lake Waccabuc, the rock outcropping with its intriguing hollows has always been called the Indian Ovens. It is much more likely that the openings were carved into the rock by the action of the water, not by prehistoric wanderers.

One can only speculate as to what this mysterious lady in black is doing as she pauses on the bridge over the channel at the end of Lake Waccabuc. Although the road looks like it leads nowhere, it is actually the highway that connected the village of South Salem with neighboring North Salem about a century ago.

Five
South Salem:
The Heart of Lewisboro

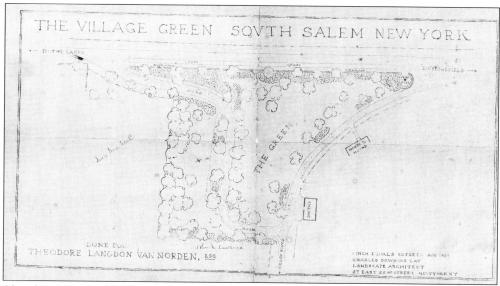

Theodore Langdon Van Norden, a prominent citizen of South Salem during the first half of the twentieth century, had grand plans for the hamlet of South Salem. He arrived in 1894, fresh from Oxford University, licensed to preach in the Presbyterian church. He served as pastor of the South Salem Presbyterian Church until 1899. A gentleman of means, he began acquiring land in the village and was involved in the development of Truesdale Lake Estates in the 1920s. In 1907, Van Norden bought the Henry Keeler homestead across the street from the church and opened an inn that he called The Horse and Hound. In conjunction with this, he obviously envisioned a New England village green for the hamlet. These plans, however, never came to fruition, but the discovery of this map shows what might have been.

Long a hamlet landmark, this home was built in 1799. In 1842, Henry Dauchy Keeler took ownership and started a blacksmith business that lasted for fifty years. In 1907, Theodore Van Norden bought the Keeler home and opened it as The Horse and Hound Inn. One can just imagine the coaches and touring cars that brought guests to the inn in its early days. It has remained a restaurant for many of the intervening years.

Following Main Street northward, one happens upon this picket fence that graced the front of the Thaddeus Keeler home just waiting for Tom Sawyer to come along. Tim Keeler remembers it was his job, as the youngest child, to clear the fence of leaves every fall, a task he tried to speed along once by setting fire to the leaves, with disastrous consequences. The Keeler home is now the Lewisboro Town House.

A row of fifty-year-old elm trees outlines the path leading along Main Street from the churchyard northward. The trees were planted by the Reverend Aaron Lindley, pastor of the South Salem Presbyterian Church from 1852–68. This photograph was taken in 1902. Needless to say, the elms have long since disappeared.

The Cyrus Hoyt cottage, which sat just south of Happy Home Flowers, was built in 1800. It was "a charming little house, of perfect proportions and the most picturesque dwelling in the village," said Theodore Van Norden in his unpublished manuscript written in 1927. Mr. Hoyt, a lame shoemaker and purveyor of tinware, traded for feathers, rags, and other commodities used by the farmer's wives. The house was removed in 1919.

Built in 1840, the lecture room of the Presbyterian church served as a chapel on weekdays and a Sunday school on Sundays. The annual town meeting and elections were held here. When the South Salem Library reorganized in 1897, the lecture room provided space for the books. Rumor has it that Horace Greeley, Elizabeth Cady Stanton, and Susan B. Anthony spoke here.

Originally established in 1799, but officially reorganized in 1897, the South Salem Library was always a focal point of the village. Members paid 50¢ dues, annually. The library was housed in the lecture room for almost seventy years. In 1964, the library books were moved to their new home in the current building next to the town house. The lecture room is now Russell Antiques.

Scenes that we take for granted today weren't always so! The lecture room, at the edge of the cemetery, was moved across Main Street in 1906. The two-story building in the background belonged to a blacksmith named Min Barrett. On the ground floor, he shoed oxen; on the second floor, he shoed horses; and on the top floor, he repaired harnesses. The lecture room now occupies the site of Min Barrett's shop.

Mary Louise Bouton was a treasured link to South Salem's past. She was a member of one of the town's founding families. Miss Bouton's Nursery School provided a proper start to learning for many generations of the town's children. She guided the lives of our youngsters until she retired in 1977, at the age of 96! Mary Louise Bouton died in 1985, nine days short of her 104th birthday.

The Thaddeus Keeler farm on Spring Street was a center of activity. The farm supplied the family's food needs, and Thad Keeler's sawmill serviced area farmers' lumber demands. On Saturday nights, the upstairs room of the mill vibrated to the sounds of the fiddle and the square dance calls of Thaddeus himself, as neighbors gathered for a favorite South Salem pastime.

Thad Keeler is dwarfed by the sawdust pile near his sawmill on Spring Street. Sawdust was a necessity for packing ice after it was cut every winter. The sawmill stood close to where the salt dome sits today. Mr. Keeler was a sawyer, a carpenter, a builder, a jack of all trades, and a good musician, to boot!

St. John's Episcopal Church was erected in 1853 at a cost of $2,550. The 30-by-48-foot fieldstone chapel was built in a picturesque grove given to the church by Stephen Hoyt and his wife, Sarah. Outdoor services had often been held in the Hoyt grove before 1853, with as many as two hundred people attending. Few changes to the structure have been made since this c. 1910 picture was taken.

The original pulpit and baptismal font grace St. John's Sanctuary. A peaceful country feeling has welcomed parishioners to Sunday services since the church was consecrated on September 18, 1855. A local quarry provided stone for the church, and the interior furnishings were made by parish members and local craftsmen.

The South Salem Presbyterian Church has been a focal point of the hamlet since 1752. This church, built in 1826, is a typical New England church. It served worshippers from a wide area extending from Ridgefield, Connecticut, to Cross River and Boutonville. In this c. 1902 photograph, the newly built church parlors are visible in the rear of the building. The churchyard contains headstones dating to 1755.

The interior of the church was refurbished in 1872. A new pulpit and extension for the organ and choir were installed at the north end of the church. The galleries were removed and the old belfry was transformed into a gallery. The walls were frescoed and elegant oval windows of ground glass replaced the double rows of square windows. A new organ was installed in 1894. This photograph was taken prior to 1902.

82

All that remained standing of this beautiful church after a devastating fire on January 30, 1973, was a ghostly facade. Of the church parlor annex, the chimney alone stood tall in front of the manse. A new church was constructed on the site with the help of the entire community. The White Church is truly a symbol of brotherhood. The third South Salem Presbyterian church was dedicated on October 19, 1975.

The church bell toppled with the steeple during the fire. Cast in 1898, it had hung in the belfry for seventy-five years. Too damaged to be rung again, the bell was rescued by the firemen and now sits in the sanctuary of the new church.

Established about the time of the Civil War, Cyrus Lawrence's general store was the village gathering place. The mail arrived by horse and wagon twice daily from Ridgefield and Katonah. Lawrence served as postmaster until his death in 1897. He was beloved by all and noted for his sense of humor and kindness. The first South Salem telephone was installed here in 1895.

"The shelves upon one side held rolls of dry goods and boxes of boots and shoes to the ceiling. Upon the other were boxes and canisters from which tea and coffee, sugar and spices were shoveled with little scoops" (from Theodore Van Norden's 1927 unpublished manuscript). The children's favorite place was the candy showcase. The store was lit by a kerosene lamp and heated by the pot-bellied stove.

Paul Black Sr. is standing in front of Allaire's Market on Main Street. The building was built in 1911 by Edward Smith, postmaster and shopkeeper in South Salem from 1897 until the 1920s. The store ceased to exist in the 1950s, but the post office continued in operation with Mrs. Reilly as postmistress until about 1960. Now a private dwelling, it is the second house north of Happy Home Flowers.

The South Salem Drama Group was organized in 1934 to "provide recreational activity in the quiet little village of South Salem." At first the plays were produced in the Truesdale Lake Clubhouse, but, by 1936, the drama group had their own theater in the Bacon Barn on Spring Street. *Who Says Can't*, their premier production in February 1935, starred Paul Black, Marion Bouton, Esther Reynolds, Elisha Keeler, Tim Keeler, and Dorothy Lowney.

Sometimes getting to church and back could be quite a struggle in the country! This horse and buggy attempted to compete with the snow banks along Bouton Road with mixed results on Easter Sunday in 1915. This photograph was marked "Halfway to Leslie Bouton's."

Road-building, South Salem style, is shown here in the late 1920s. Thaddeus Keeler and crew are at work blasting a rock ledge along Spring Street, near St. John's Episcopal Church, so that the road can be straightened and widened to accommodate increased automobile traffic.

Lassen's South Salem Inn serves as a backdrop for this photograph of William Bepler, grandson of Heinrich and Johanna Lassen. Young William poses on his dad's first car in the early 1930s. The Lassens operated the South Salem Inn until the early '50s, when Jack Hilbert bought the property. The mansard-roof house, similar to the Tator home, was demolished about 1970, when the Bouton Road Mobil Station was built.

Sunday drives to the country were what America was all about in the first decades of the twentieth century. The state road from Cross River to the Connecticut line went through South Salem. Heinrich Lassen's South Salem Inn, at the corner of Bouton Road and the state highway, was a popular stopping place. Gasoline pumps and a roadside ice cream stand replenished both car and driver.

Clattercote Farm, the Boardman family home, stood on Old Oscaleta Road, just west of the Connecticut line. David Pardee built the house *c.* 1815. According to the unpublished Van Norden manuscript, "the burning of the house in 1924 was a great loss to South Salem, for it possessed unusual charm." Robert Boardman, now in his eighties, remembers the "all day car excursions from Riverdale" to visit his grandmother in the country.

The North District School, built *c.* 1822, stood on land donated by Stephen Gilbert. The school was better known as the Red Bridge Academy, a title suggested by the red wooden bridge located nearby that crossed the Coal Kiln Brook. The school sat in a meadow called Lime Kiln Lot southeast of the bridge. Pictured are the scholars of 1881. The Red Bridge Academy closed in 1940.

In 1857, three existing school districts were combined to form South Salem School District #3, and this elegant, two-story, two-classroom schoolhouse was constructed on land purchased from Stephen Hoyt. The school is still standing behind the Salem Market on Spring Street and is now a private home. In 1953, a fire in the house killed the weaver living there at the time. This photograph was taken c. 1890.

Teacher Ethel Storm, second from the left in the top row, poses with her pupils in this September 21, 1921 school picture. The group is standing in front of the District #3 School. Families represented include the Keelers, Tators, Sfondrinis, Scofields, Blacks, Stones, Brouses, Hawleys, and Janeskys; many of these were founding families of South Salem.

Consolidation, first proposed in 1919, was a long time aborning. Construction of the South Salem Union Free School on Bouton Road began in 1939 at a cost of $150,000. The first classes met in 1940. The building was designed to incorporate the feeling of the five consolidated districts with five teachers serving grades one through eight. Kindergarten was added in 1945. The era of the one-room schoolhouse in Lewisboro ended in 1940.

Mary Mazza (right) was "queen of the kitchen" at South Salem School, now Lewisboro School, back when school lunches were truly "homemade." Mary and Esther Tripp (left) are preparing a Halloween feast, probably in the late 1940s or early '50s. Mrs. Mazza was also famous for her town highway department Christmas parties!

Conceived as a year-round recreational community in the early 1930s, Truesdale Lake Estates offered fishing, swimming, boating, and tennis for its homeowner members. Home to one of the first official Sailfish (later Sunfish) fleets, the weekend sailing races were a beautiful sight. Truesdale Lake was formed by the damming of a pond outlet on the Keeler farm in the 1920s. This photograph was taken in front of the Koenig property *c.* 1954.

What's a lake for, if not fishing? John Blair (left) and his brother-in-law, Bill Speckanbach, show off a 5-pound, large-mouth bass. The catch was the largest one reported for Truesdale Lake until that time. The photograph was taken about 1952.

Local legend whispers that this building belonged to Dutch Schultz during Prohibition. In the early 1940s, Enzo Yocca purchased the Spring Street property for his South Salem Studios, where miniatures and military training devices were manufactured during World War II. South Salem Studios continued to produce military strategic identification ships and aircraft models, topographical globes, and rocket trajectory models until 1962.

Enzo Yocca, an Italian marquis, studied architecture at the Sorbonne before immigrating to America. He and his wife, Lillian Kennedy Yocca, were miniature makers extraordinaire. Wilhemena Kennedy, Mrs. Yocca's sister, added her artistic expertise to the enterprise. Daughter Maddalena Yocca contributed her talents to the family business, too.

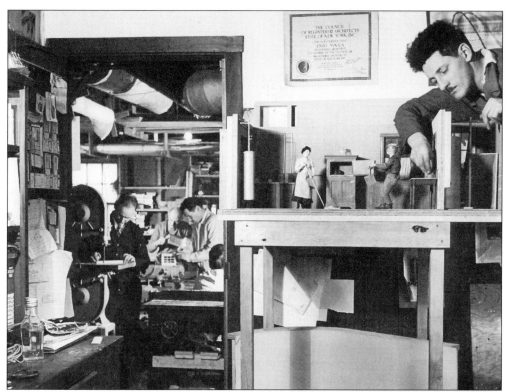

No idle hands were found at South Salem Studios! The gentleman in the foreground is adjusting one of the Yocca dioramas that was displayed at the 1939 World's Fair for the General Electric "History of Refrigeration" exhibit. The studios produced a number of advertising displays for corporations like Pepperell Fabrics and Alexander Smith Carpets. Master craftsman Yocca can be seen at work in the studio background.

The assembly line at South Salem Studios employed as many as seventy local men and women around the clock during World War II. They produced scale models of American, German, and Japanese ships for training and identification purposes for the navy and war departments. Models were manufactured from metal and wood in accurate detail, including the guns and rigging. Artisans worked in scales of: 1: 500, 1: 1,200, and 1: 2,000.

George Tator and Sons' Dodge was one of the original dealerships in the U.S. Tator sold seven touring cars in 1914, his first year, for $785 each. He began his business with collateral of $800 and a horse in a rented barn next to his family's home. Over the next few years, he added a repair shop and the roadside filling station visible in this 1941 photograph.

George Tator sponsored a race team in the early days of dirt track competition. Charlie Ganung of Katonah was Tator's champion driver in his Miller #4. The team was well known on the northeastern circuit. This particular racing car was bought from fellow racer Ralph DePalma with the stipulation that Ganung would not race the car against DePalma for one year. This photograph was taken in the late 1920s or early '30s.

The water tower on Farvue Farm, one of South Salem's landmarks, was built about 1900 by Thaddeus Keeler and Edward Weeks. This photograph, taken a few years after the tower was finished, shows the windmill that once sat atop the 60-foot tower. Leo Gustafson of Cross River recalls how he used to start the gasoline engine that powered the water pump every morning on his way to work at Tator's Garage.

South Salem has had its share of disastrous fires, such as this 1962 blaze that destroyed a Farvue Farm barn belonging to former Vice President Henry A. Wallace, an experimental farmer by avocation. Vice President Wallace bred chickens, and the incubators were on the first floor of this building. The fire started in mid-afternoon and lasted until dark. Many chickens were lost in the fire.

Henry Agard Wallace was secretary of agriculture and vice president during the Franklin D. Roosevelt administrations. In 1946, after his retirement from government, he moved to South Salem. For twenty years he maintained an experimental farm called Farvue Farm. He attempted to breed a chicken that would be both a productive egg-layer and a good eating chicken. Wallace was also interested in hybridizing green miniature gladioli and in crossing the French wild strawberry with a strong American berry, combining the exquisite taste with a sturdy plant that could be sold commercially. Henry Wallace was the champion of the common man, and a firm believer that most of the world's problems could be helped by making sure that the world's starving people were fed. He believed that America had the power and resources to accomplish that goal. Henry Agard Wallace died in 1965, a victim of Lou Gehrig's Disease.

Six
Lewisboro Hamlet:
The Hidden Treasure

Lewisboro Hamlet has always been somewhat elusive. Only the folks who have lived in the area all their lives seem to know its boundaries, and, even then, opinions differ. It was once an area of large dairy farms and undeveloped tracts of land. There is no longer a village. Once there was a schoolhouse, a chapel, a post office, and a store, but memories of them have long faded away. The remnants of a mill can be seen along the Mill River, and the bed of a railroad that never came is visible along the Mill River and the road to Ridgefield. However, Lewisboro Hamlet is alive and well, and its residents are staunchly proud of who they are! Life was different in the 1940s, when this Fourth of July celebration was captured on film in the skies over Lake Kitchawan. Fireworks were legal then, and you could buy whatever kind you wanted at the local gas stations. Each summer the Lake Kitchawan community celebrated the holiday in a spectacular way.

Charles and Jane Davis enjoy the sunshine in the unique entryway to their son Theodore's home. The Davis house was on the northwest corner of Shady Lane and Elmwood "Avenue" (as the old-timers say). The house is no longer there, having been removed many years ago.

Willis (age 19), Grace (age 15), Charles (age 7), and Kenneth (age 4), the grandchildren of Charles and Jane Davis, pose for a picture in the yard of the Theodore Davis home about 1908. Young Charles's daughter, Helen D. Worden, remembers transplanting old-fashioned roses from this property long after the house had ceased to exist, and she still enjoys the fragrance of the roses in her own Connecticut garden more than fifty years later.

In the early 1900s, life moved at a slower pace in Lewisboro. The horse and buggy, not the automobile, was the primary means of transportation on our dirt roads. Frances Duryea Scott and her mother, Susan Duryea, are ready for a drive on a fine summer day. The Stephen Duryea homestead, pictured here, is just north of Beck's Hill Cemetery.

The more hands during haying season, the better! Before mechanical balers, the hay had to be raked and gathered by hand on Lewisboro farms. In this c. 1915 photograph, the members of the Stephen Duryea family are working together to get the hay into the barn on their New Canaan Road homestead (at least, they will be working when they finish having their picture taken!).

It's corn husking time in this early photograph from the Stephen Duryea family collection. Frances Duryea and a couple of helpers are showing off part of the field corn crop for the camera. Every farmer planted enough field corn to feed the family livestock over the winter. The animals were often the most valuable possessions the family owned.

The hamlet of Lewisboro lies within the area known as the Oblong. The Olmstead house, at the corner of Elmwood Road and West Lane, probably dates to the mid-1700s. The Olmsteads were early settlers in Ridgefield. When the Oblong dispute was settled, this property was transferred from Connecticut to New York. In the early 1940s, the Armistead family purchased the Olmstead house, about the time this photograph was taken.

There wasn't much leisure time in a farm family household, but Sundays could offer an afternoon off to relax with a game of croquet, or time to pose for a group picture. The Morgan family lived on Mill River Road in what is now the Augenti home.

Lots of sun and just the right amount of rain was what the farmers wanted, and needed. It looks like this corn crop is more than knee high, so it must be past the Fourth of July! Lewisboro families were self-sufficient well into the twentieth century. Growing enough food to feed the family and the livestock was important to them.

Lucy Raymond was a well-known Lewisboro resident in the first half of the twentieth century. She owned a small farm on Elmwood Road near the former John Lewis homestead, later the Episcopalian rectory. Lucy sold eggs and milk to neighbors and to Sunday visitors from the city. When her hens weren't laying in abundance, Miss Lucy would resort to "borrowing" fresh eggs from a store in Stamford, to sell them as her own! She also sold unpasteurized milk back when such a thing was allowed. Later on, when restrictions were put on the selling of raw milk, Lucy Raymond would leave a milk can on her porch and customers would take what they needed, leaving a "donation" in its place.

Walter and Alice Lane Poor's country home on Elmwood Road was named Onatru Farm by Alice's father, Edward Lane, when he bought the property in 1904. Note the young evergreen trees in front of the stone wall in the field across from the house. These trees were planted by Alice's husband, Walter, in the 1930s. He was a great lover of trees, although he preferred living in the city to life in the country.

This photograph taken prior to 1931 shows the Onatru Farm as a working farm. A buttery and a milk separator were housed in the cellar of the superintendent's cottage, pictured here. Enough butter was made to supply the family and several Ridgefield restaurants. The water tower stands over an artesian well, storing water for use on the farm. Ice cut from the Raymond pond was stored in the closest small outbuilding..

Alice Lane Poor inherited Onatru Farm in 1924. The Poor family lived in New York City but spent summers and holidays in Lewisboro. They loved Onatru and kept it as a working farm, under the able management of Rufus "Rufe" Green. The farm supplied the family's dairy and food needs. The Poors were active on many town committees and in the World War II war effort. They also were major contributors to town community service organizations like the Vista Fire Department. In 1978, Alice Poor donated Onatru Farm to the town for use as a park "to preserve the rural atmosphere" of the town of Lewisboro. She died in 1981 at the age of 96. Walter died in 1945.

Walter S. Poor Jr. has found the perfect place to read a favorite book in this 1923 photograph. Walter is reading under the huge butternut tree near the kitchen. The Poor family spent summers and holidays at Onatru Farm until about 1940, when they moved to Lewisboro from Manhattan permanently.

Grace T. Poor, riding on Brownie, her brother's pony, is inspecting the playhouse in the north field near the main house. Grace loved all the animals on the farm, especially the horses and the dogs. She shared her mother's enthusiasm for farming and loved to take an active part, often driving the farm machinery as she was growing up. The playhouse is no longer there.

Farm manager Rufus Green, Grace Poor (center), and a friend are "on a roll" around the fields, pulled by Lady and Dick. "Rufe" worked on the farm from the 1920s until his death in 1962. He kept detailed diaries about life on the farm in the 1940s and 1950s. Grace claims, "He could pick up a 100-pound sack of feed with his teeth!"

It's summertime and haying is the order of the day. You had to make hay while the sun was shining, and Grace Poor is walking Brownie through the field with the hay rake. During haying season, everyone's help was needed. The first tractor was purchased in 1942, but the hay was not baled mechanically on Onatru Farm until after 1946.

Onatru was typical of the farms in Lewisboro that made each family fairly self-sufficient. This picture of the hog shed was taken about the time the Lanes purchased the property in 1904. The shed was located in the north field, across the driveway from the main house.

The sheep are enjoying the sunshine behind the cow barn at Onatru in this early 1940s photograph. Kept mostly for meat, perhaps this group is waiting to be shorn. Grace Poor Frost remembers the time someone tried to shear the sheep with the horse clippers. That certainly didn't work!

Farm work follows the seasons. Rufe Green and Grace Poor are hard at work rolling the back field, north of the lane, next to the woods. Slow and steady and patient, the team pulling the roller knew its job. The fields that were so carefully cultivated by crop rotation during the 1930s and '40s are now town athletic fields.

Oops! Missed that curve! Even today, the corner of the New Canaan Road (Route 123) and Mill River Road is a challenge to motorists. This car seems to have missed the bridge over the Mill River completely. The town highway crew was enlisted to retrieve the unfortunate automobile from the water. Rumor has it that this spot provided great eel fishing in the "good ol' days"!

On October 20, 1955, a heavy-hitting northeaster hit the Lewisboro area with a vengeance. Power was knocked out, and the Mill River was so swollen by the heavy rainfall that the dam was broken through and angry waters spilled out of the mill pond along the Mill River Road near the intersection with Lake Kitchawan Drive.

The October 20, 1955 storm caused major highway damage throughout the town. Five bridges were washed out, including the Mill River Road bridge. This storm followed the wettest August in history, during which Hurricane Diane dropped 6 inches of rain on the town on August 18th. In this photograph, Ron Egloff and a friend survey the damage to their neighborhood.

"Duz does everything!" Popular commercials and the soap operas seem to have inspired this "queen of the clothesline," who, in reality, is little Miss Bohannon. Her father is adjusting her clothesline, making ready for a Lake Kitchawan costume parade in the early '40s. Note the Connecticut license plate. For many years Lewisboro Hamlet residents had Connecticut mailing addresses, so they qualified for Connecticut license plates.

Dressing up in costume is a lot of fun for these Lake Kitchawan children, but posing for the camera can be a little scary, as evidenced by the faces on a few of the masqueraders. Judging by the vintage of the cars, this parade probably took place in the early 1940s. Can you find a relative, quite possibly your grandparent, among the marchers?

The Lake Kitchawan Association Beach Committee relaxes in the clubhouse after a summer affair. Mrs. Ed Griswald, at the far left, and Mrs. Bohannon, fourth from the left, were two members of this group. Lake Kitchawan Park was formed in 1925 from two parcels of land: part of Southeastern Farms, at the southern end of the lake; and part of the Craft property, at the north end of the spring-fed lake.

Many carnivals, clambakes, and bake sales were held by the Lake Kitchawan Association to raise money to purchase a clubhouse. The money was finally raised, and the clubhouse became a reality in 1951. The carnivals were held in the field across from the beach which is now a community garden area.

AIRPLANE OBSERVATION VOLUNTEER

name to be typed here

During World War II, patriotism in the town of Lewisboro was high. The Lewisboro Airplane Observation Post went into action on December 9, 1941. Service was discontinued on March 28, 1942, because of the proximity of several other facilities. The post operated on a 24-hour-a-day schedule with two-person teams working three-hour shifts. Plane watchers came from all parts of town to the observation tower on the E.J. Horwath estate on Elmwood Road. Code named "Dudley," the Lewisboro lookout reported all planes flying over the area. When a plane was spotted, a FLASH message was phoned to the army command post indicating type, altitude, direction, etc. The statistics for the four months of plane spotting were: December '41, 562 planes; January '42, 607 planes; February '42, 687 planes; and March '42, 725 planes. Patriotic citizen volunteers numbered 285. No enemy planes were reported, however. This sketch was to be used for a business-card-sized ID for the volunteers.

Seven

Vista:
A View to the Past

The commuters who whiz by today would not recognize this corner as the intersection of Route 123 and East Street. Ninety years ago, when this photograph was taken, the corner of Smith Ridge Road (New Canaan Road) and East Street suggested a less hurried atmosphere. The "commuters" were the Lewisboro and Vista farmers in their wagons on their way to New Canaan or Norwalk to deliver farm produce and milk to the markets, or to purchase needed supplies. The Vista Schoolhouse sat in the meadow behind the road sign. Children from the school drew water from a well near the corner house pictured here. Vista residents were farmers, for the most part. In the winter they did piece work at the Fancher Shoe Factory above the general store. There were several saw and gristmills and a quarry near East Street. There has always been a strong affinity between the families of Vista and New Canaan, Connecticut, since they share a common border.

The Vista Schoolhouse on the corner of East Street and the New Canaan Road was built c. 1870, replacing an older building that stood opposite the Vista Market. It was typical of the time, with separate entrances for boys and girls. Students had to supply their own slates, paper, and pencils. The school was used until 1940, when South Salem School opened, consolidating all the town's school districts.

The following excerpt is taken from a letter written by Jared Sparks Pidgeon, whose mother, Helen Sparks, attended the Vista Schoolhouse from 1885–1890. "Weather was no excuse for absenteeism. Some zero-minus days the children wore their coats and gloves all day as the woodstove never brought the room up to a comfortable temperature." This c. 1920s photograph shows the interior of the schoolhouse with the pot-bellied stove, front and center!

Mrs. Helen Valien was one of the last teachers in the Vista Schoolhouse. She is standing in the doorway in this 1936 school photograph. Most students from the era of the one-room school praised the teacher's efforts and treasured the extra knowledge they absorbed by listening to another grade's lessons.

Asa Crawford was the schoolmaster at the Vista Schoolhouse c. 1875. He owned a farm in East Woods, about 3 miles from the school. During the noon hour break, he would rush home, do his farm chores, and get back in time for the afternoon session.

Rufe Smith and his wife, Catherine, had a large dairy farm in Vista that extended along both sides of New Canaan Road, just north of the Vista Market. Although it is said that Rufe could be a bit on the irascible side, neighboring children bravely gathered the tastiest blueberries in Vista from his meadows. This photograph was taken c. 1930, when the Smiths were in their nineties.

Peter Smith built this house in the mid-nineteenth century. His son, Rufus, inherited the property and operated a dairy farm for many years. The Vista Post Office was located in the front room of the house from 1887 to 1902. Rufe gave out the mail and sold butter, milk, and cream at the same time.

In the early twentieth century, the Van Name home on East Street was a general store. The front room housed the groceries, another smaller room contained the animal feed, and in the back portion of the house, a pool hall provided a gathering place for the local menfolk in the evenings. Ed Smith lived upstairs over his grandfather's store and has many fond memories, especially of the candy case!

There were several Fitch families in Vista. Chester Fitch operated a sawmill on East Street. The sawmill stood near the unmarked Fitch family cemetery. Except for the little sticker in the corner of this photograph stating, "Friends from Vista. Aunt Sara Fitch," the identity of the family in this carefully posed c. 1890 photograph is unknown. Could one of the gentlemen possibly be sawyer Chester Fitch?

Just visible in the foreground is the platform of the Vista General Store. Sometime later, the platform was removed and the store was moved back from the road. Hidden in the trees across from the church, a building is barely visible. This may be the church of a breakaway temperance group from the Vista Methodist Episcopal Church. The church was later moved to East Woods, some say.

In this view of the Vista Methodist Episcopal Church, a corn field is visible between the church and the market. Since the loading platform of the store cannot be seen, this may be a later photograph than the previous one. The church was built c. 1857 and was served, for most of its years, by a circuit minister. In 1972, the Stevens Memorial United Methodist Church was built, and this old church was sold.

The cornerstone for St. Paul's Episcopal Chapel was laid in 1871, but the church was not erected until the late 1890s with funds bequeathed by John Lewis. Consecrated on June 12, 1900, as the Rockwell Memorial Chapel of St. Paul, the chapel was named in honor of Gould Rockwell, a parish benefactor. The chapel boasts a Tiffany window and a bell donated by "Boss" William Tweed of New York City. At one time, there were horse sheds on the property so that the teams waiting for the churchgoers could stay dry during inclement weather. Alice Poor used to play the organ for Sunday services with the help of her son, Walter, or another parish lad, to pump the instrument.

Beck's Hill Cemetery sits in a shaded setting across the road from St. Paul's Chapel. The cemetery is a town cemetery, not associated with the church. The origin of the name is unknown and there are no Becks buried there. The earliest burial inscription date is 1805. John Lewis, the town's namesake, is buried there next to his mother.

Dr. Bryan of Ridgefield was responsible for the New Canaan Development Corporation's idea of "affordable housing." In the 1930s, a string of "Tobacco Road" tarpaper shacks stood where the Vista Shopping Center is today. It was a great relief to Vista residents when the houses were torn down. It is said that Dr. Bryan built the poorly constructed homes in protest when the town refused to let him erect stores on the property.

Betsy Munroe Beers, daughter Julia, and Ambrose Beers pose for a family portrait in front of the West Road homestead built by Ambrose in 1844. Ownership of the classic story-and-a-half farmhouse has remained in the Beers family since 1844. Hans Bauer, Ambrose's great-great grandson, and his family live there at present.

It's not often we can glimpse inside an older home and witness "the way things used to be!" Here is a turn-of-the-century peek at the rocker waiting by the shiny kitchen stove, and, beyond that, into the front bedroom. Modern times have come to the Ambrose Beers homestead.

Mud Pond, also known as Tom Mead Pond, and Siskowit Lake were popular fishing holes and gathering places for Vista folks. This photograph of Lester and Alice Beers in their first car offers a glimpse of Mud Pond in its glory days.

Life's pleasures were simpler in the early 1900s. Alice Beers (Bauer) and her mother, Alice D. Beers, row out onto Mud Pond, a beautiful lake that stretches from the East Woods area into New Canaan. It looks like young Alice has got her mind set on a fish for dinner! The lake is now part of the Stamford Water Supply System.

Once the automobile started taking over the country roads as the vehicle of choice, literally running the horse and buggy off the highway by the 1920s, gas stations and garages replaced the corner blacksmith. Jack Nicolai, seen in this photograph from the late 1920s, managed the Lewisboro Garage at the corner of West Road and Smith Ridge Road (Route 123) for many years.

Next door to the Lewisboro Garage, Jack Nicolai's wife, Bertha, and friend Stella Mead offered homemade cookies, candies, pies, and jellies for sale to the passing travelers. The stand was open in the summertime only. On some days young Miss Katherine Nicolai (Baker) would help her mother tend to business at the roadside stand.

On March 5 and 6, 1940, an ice storm struck the area, and Vista was devastated. Seventeen successive telephone poles along Smith Ridge Road, beginning near West Road, were toppled by the weight of the ice. Needless to say, electrical service was disrupted for several days.

Snowstorms always seem to bring out the cameras! Lester Beers took a photographic pause for posterity as he shoveled out his driveway on West Road after a heavy winter storm in the 1940s. In this neck of the woods, when there was this much snow, families got out the skis and went cross country to the Vista Market for emergency supplies.

Looking rather forlorn after the effects of the March 1940 ice storm, this building saw many rollicking times as a dance pavilion and roadside stand. The establishment was owned by the Peterson family and was one of the many popular watering holes during Prohibition. Vista and Lewisboro, tucked away in Westchester's elbow, were often "overlooked" by the constabulary, which made for some wild times. Peterson's is now a kennel.

Baseball has always been a favorite pastime in our town. The Vista Bobcats team was the pride of Vista in the 1940s and 1950s. The champions pictured here are Barton Waite, Charles "Pug" Wood, Bill Raymond, John Jordan, Cloyd Bobletz, Bill Westcott, Ralph Jordan, Huck Waterbury, Robert Reynolds, Robert Bobletz, and Al Jordan. The tale is told that the team won a magnificent twenty-seven games in a row!

The Vista Fire Department was organized in 1941. The first firehouse was on the corner of Blueberry Lane in a former tavern. In 1954, fire devastated the renovated building, destroying two firetrucks. Charter member Ed Smith, with forty years of hindsight, opined, "It was the best thing that ever happened, since the new firehouse is a building the community can take pride in!"

The women's auxiliary of the Vista Fire Department was established on August 12, 1948. The members of the auxiliary sponsored fund-raisers and social events in support of the fire department. An early photograph shows the group gathered for a dinner at the Hayloft Restaurant in South Salem.

126

In this *c.* 1909 photograph, we can see how Vista got its name. On a clear day, the old-timers say a farmer could see all the way to Long Island Sound, about 10 miles to the east. The fields were kept cleared of trees and brush for the benefit of the crops and animals. Stone fences and fields filled much of the landscape, leaving a lot of open space for dreamers and doers.

Acknowledgments

This book is the result of the efforts of many people interested in keeping alive the history of the town of Lewisboro. Almost forty families, individuals, and organizations contributed photographs to the project. In many instances, attics and closets were searched and old memories were resurrected along with the dusty family photograph albums, all because of a request from my unfamiliar voice on the telephone asking for information and photographs. This project gave me the opportunity to meet many wonderful folks eager to open doors to Lewisboro's past.

My project could not have been successful without the gracious sharing of memories by several descendants of Lewisboro's founding families, namely, Lois and Joyce Reynolds, Evelyn Russell, Judith and David Moore, Susan Henry, Timothy Keeler, Elisha and Lois Keeler, Hans and Ruth Bauer, and Helen Davis Worden.

Equally valuable were the reminiscences of families who have called Lewisboro home for almost a century: Charles Tator, Waldie and Barbara Gullin, Henry Palmer, Edward Smith, Edna Waite, Pearl Whitman, Connie Bobletz, and Grace Poor Frost.

Add to these the individuals who are relative newcomers to town over the last seventy years: Katherine Baker, Maddalena Yocca, Captain Guirey, Karen Armistead, Laurie Bepler, Frieda Halpern, Mac Arons, Dorothy and Jack Benish, Irene and John Blair, Ron Eglof, Reverend Harold Quigley, Stephen Hoyt, Christina and Fred Cowles, the Michael Stillman family, the Thomas Wright family, the Augenti family, and the family of Henry A. Wallace.

My sincere thanks to the South Salem Library, the South Salem Fire Department, the Lake Katonah Association, and to Beth Herr, curator of the Ward Pound Ridge Reservation Trailside Museum, for access to their photograph collections.

Several quotes have been cited from the Van Norden manuscript, an unpublished, extensively documented history of South Salem compiled by Theodore Langdon Van Norden in 1927. This source is available, for research purposes, at the South Salem Library.

I am grateful for the organizational help of Jackie Pamenter and Gail Daigle. Invaluable photographic assistance was rendered by Timothy Keeler and Robert LeBlond, Hans Bauer, and Ellen Meagher.

Supplementing the photograph collection of the town historian was the collection of old photographs of the Three Lakes area belonging to Arthur Holden, which was made available by Kenneth Soltesz, who offered his assistance in many ways.

In bringing this project to a close, I must acknowledge the patience and understanding of my family who will now regain the use of the living room!

I hope this book is only a start, that it will make the public aware of the wealth that lies forgotten in trunks and boxes and attics everywhere. Perhaps it will encourage people to sort through their own photograph collections and add their family's history to the ongoing story of Lewisboro.